The pictures tell the story of the death of a parent in a simple but moving way. Adolescents and adults with learning difficulties (mental handicap) will find the pictures are meaningful with or without the text. The book will help to inform readers about the simple facts of death and about feelings of grief. For bereaved readers the story may parallel their own experience. Parents, friends or professionals will be able to help them share their own story of loss, and guide them to new hope in their own futures — just as the story ends on an optimistic note. The story begins and ends in the family photograph album, and readers are encouraged to turn to their own album later.

When Dad Died

Sheila Hollins
Lester Sireling
Illustrated by Elizabeth Webb

St George's Hospital Medical School
LONDON
in association with
Silent Books
CAMBRIDGE

First Published in Great Britain 1989
by St George's Hospital Medical School, Cranmer Terrace, Tooting,
London SW17 0RE
in association with Silent Books, Swavesey, Cambridge CB4 5RA

© Text and illustration copyright Sheila Hollins and Lester Sireling 1989

ISBN 1 85183 019 7

Typeset by Goodfellow & Egan, Cambridge

Printed and bound in Great Britain by
HGA Printing Company Ltd. Brentford Middlesex

To our parents and our children.

With thanks to the following people whose interest and encouragement has made this book possible: Nigel Hollins, Joan Bicknell, Enid Fairhead, Freda Macey and Sue Redshaw.

This is a picture of Stephen with his family. The story tells us what happened when his Dad died.

One day Dad had a pain.

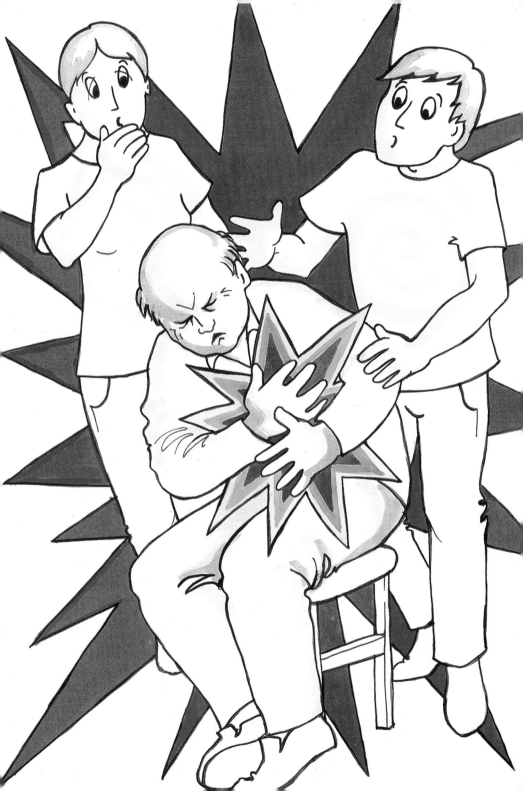

Mum phoned 999 for an ambulance.

The ambulance came quickly and took Dad to hospital.

Mum, Stephen and Julie went to the hospital to see Dad.

They bought some flowers to cheer him up.

Dad was in bed because he was ill.
A nurse was looking after him.

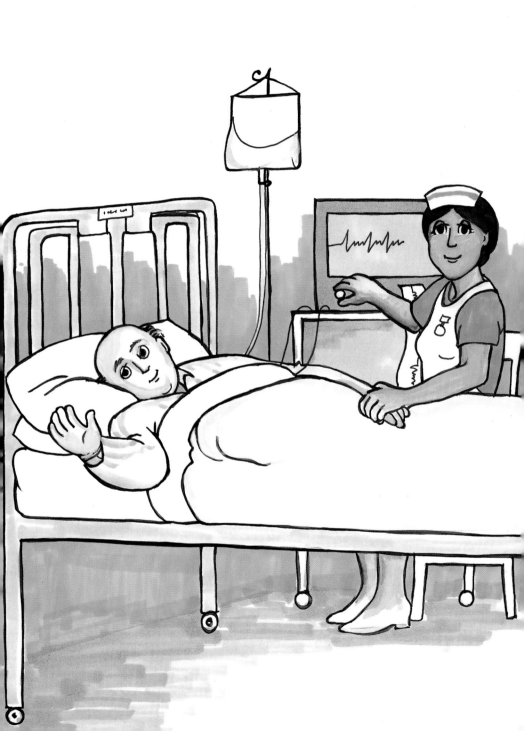

Dad was happy to see them.
They didn't know what to say.
Soon Dad got tired.
That was because he was ill.

Mum said it was time to go.
They waved goodbye to Dad.

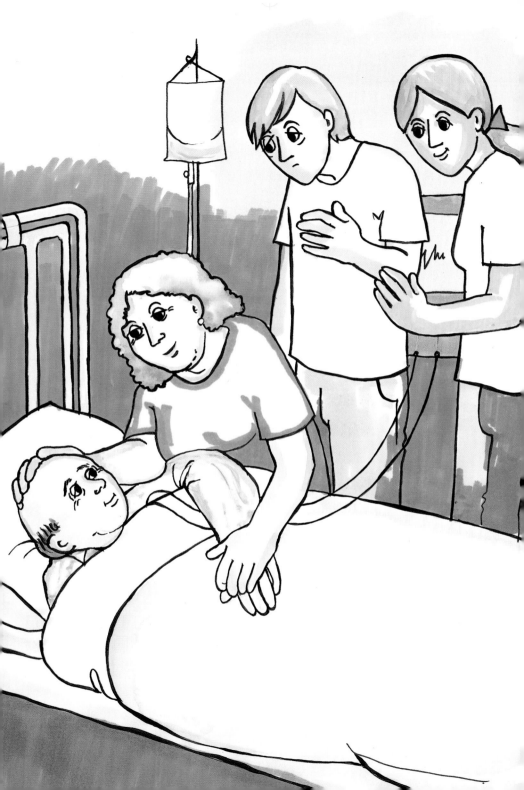

Mum said "Let's turn off the television and talk about Dad." Stephen didn't feel like talking. He just wanted Dad to get better.

Dad was very ill.
He slept most of the time.
Stephen sat next to his bed.
He wanted to be with his Dad.
Sometimes his Dad woke up and
looked at him.

Stephen kissed his Dad.
He wanted to say goodbye.

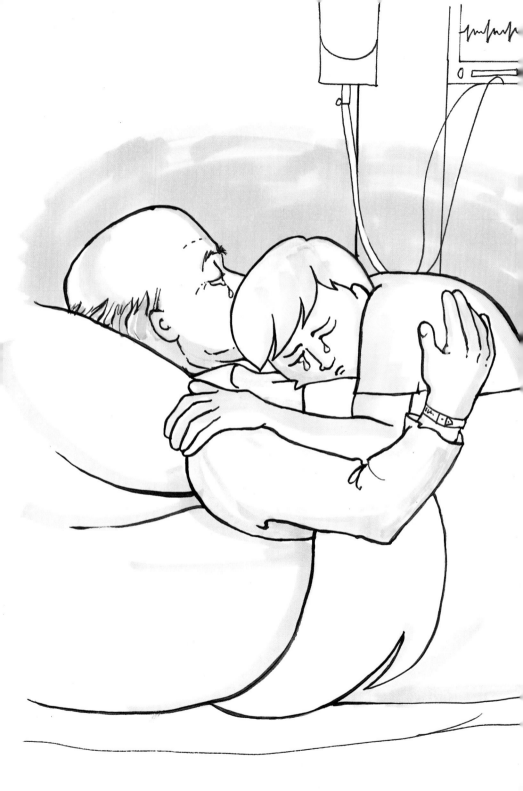

Mum said "I'm worried about Dad. I don't think he'll get better."

Later Dad died.
He was not asleep.
He had stopped breathing.
He couldn't walk or talk
or see anymore.

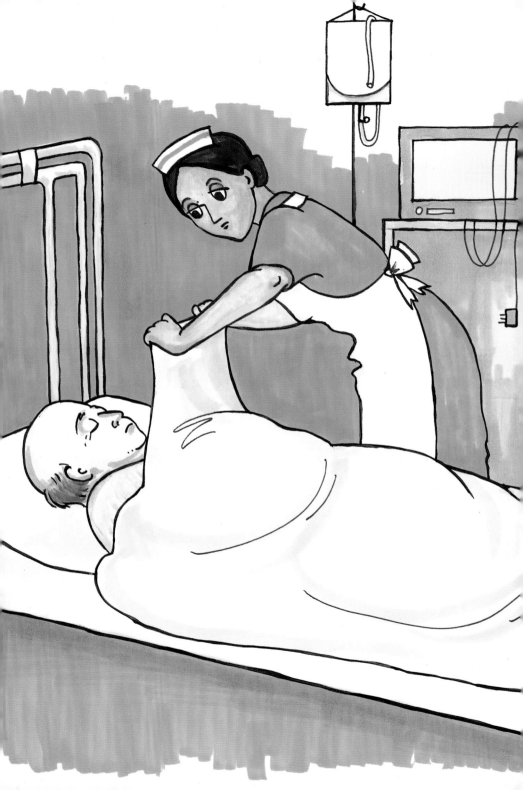

The nurse phoned Mum and told
her that Dad had died.
Mum was very upset.

Mum woke Stephen up.
She had something very sad to
tell him.
"Dad won't come home again.
He died last night."

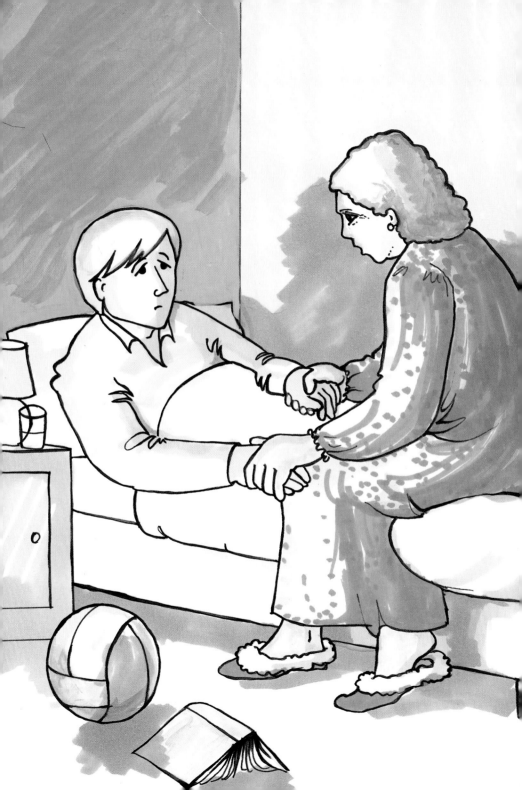

Stephen thought it was a mistake.
He wanted to go to the hospital to
see Dad.
Mum wouldn't let him go and they
had an argument.

Stephen and Julie didn't
feel hungry.
They both felt upset.

Stephen felt cross and muddled.
He still didn't believe his Dad was
dead.

Mum knew why he was angry.
She told him again that Dad
was dead.
Stephen still didn't understand.

Next day they went to see Dad.
His body was in a coffin.
Then Stephen understood that he
was dead.

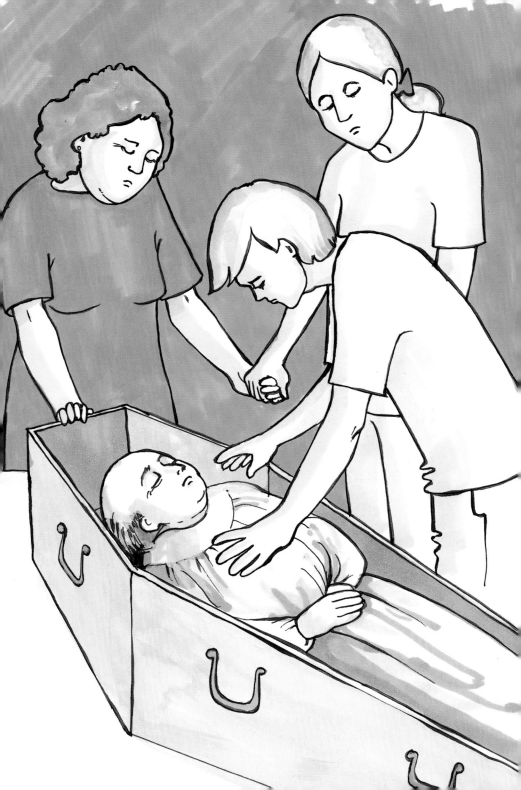

Dad's coffin was driven to
the cemetery.
Stephen, Julie and their Mum came
in a different car.
Dad's friends came to say goodbye.

Everyone said goodbye to Dad.
Stephen wondered why Dad
had died.
Was Dad with God?

The curtains closed.
Then Dad's body was cremated
until only ashes were left.

Sometimes Stephen felt lonely.
He didn't want to play with
his friends.
They didn't know what to say.
They were glad it was not their Dad
who had died.

Stephen and Julie planted a rose bush with Dad's name on it.

Mum gave Stephen and Julie a
photograph of Dad to keep.
Stephen felt sad all over again.
Mum told Stephen that Dad wanted
him to have his watch.
That made him feel happy.

They were still a family.
They had good times together, and
they often talked about Dad.